D1648456

ANOTHER
SCROLL

Amy G. S. A. Brooks

Defiant
Readings for
Lectionary
Year C

ANOTHER
SCROLL

The Pilgrim Press, 700 Prospect Avenue East
Cleveland, Ohio 44115-1100
thepilgrimpress.com

Published 2021.

Scripture quotations, unless otherwise noted, are from the New Revised Standard Version of the Bible, © 1989 by the Division of Christian Education of the National Council of Churches of Christ in the United States of America. Used by permission. Changes have been made for inclusivity.

Printed on acid-free paper.

25 24 23 22 21   1 2 3 4 5

Library of Congress Cataloging-in-Publication Data on file
LCCN: 2021936576

ISBN 978-0-8298-2177-2 (paper)
ISBN 978-0-8298-2184-0 (ebook)

Printed in The United States of America.

For Laurie, Laura, and Oliver
because they told me so.

Introduction

Beloved,

You have been told that the whole earth is full of the glory of God. Has no one ever reminded you that you too belong to this earth; and that, consequently, you too are divinely glorious?

You have been told to remove your shoes on holy ground.
Has no one ever encouraged you to sit, child-like, and sift the sand through your fingers; to build castles from these grains of truth?

You have been told to study the ancient texts.
Has no one ever given you permission to read and to keep on reading until you find yourself between the pages?

You have been given a sacred invitation to open the scripture and allow it to unfurl with courage and creativity. In many ways this mirrors the way that you unwind out to your true self as you discover and embrace your own complex identity.

You are the scroll. You are another scroll, a new scroll. The whole of creation waited with bated breath for your arrival. Your very existence is a testament to the Unknown, to the unfolding of Mystery lived out through you as organic parchment.

The Universe has called you into being and named you 'good.' You are entirely complete, a sacrosanct and inviolable person. You, yes you with the full richness of all your sacred diversities.

Beloved, in case no one has told you,

you are whole,
you are holy,
you are wholly loved.

Please be advised that this book contains language and addresses topics that some people may find traumatic. To support your mental and emotional wellbeing a list of content warnings has been incorporated into the index.

Contents

First Sunday of Advent

Night and day we pray most earnestly that we may see you face to
face and restore whatever is lacking in your faith.
1 Thessalonians 3:10

Hope

You are in the trenches.

You are in the battlefield,
in the thick of the fight.
You have shells falling around you
day and night,
kicking up dust and destruction
and a kind of death
until even noon is overcast with gloom.

Of course you can't find the sun.

It's ugly, and hard
and it hurts
in a way that feels impossible to bear
here in the trenches.

But,
turn your head to the left or to the right—
can you find one of us?

Because this is our true mission:
to slide down into the trenches
with the wounded
and be the sun.
Will you allow us to love you like that?

Maybe it will be enough for now,
when the battle is at its thickest,
to feel fingers curl around yours
and rub your hands until a spark forms,
until hope blooms
in the rich darkness of this soil,
until you are restored to knowing

that you are loved completely,
right where you are,
right here,
in the trenches.

Second Sunday of Advent

> ... and all flesh shall see the salvation of God. Luke 3:6

Peace

Her holy temple is not as shiny
      as it once was.

Her ark, transported now in a rusted cart,
contains more practical items
      than tablets of stone.

Her pillar of cloud is only seen
      sporadically,
on the rare occasion
She can beg, borrow, or steal
a cigarette.

She makes Her home now
among litter,
trash and scraps of charity
the only sacrifices
laid upon Her altar.

She calls the people,
as She has always done,
to follow Her.

She cries out, disturbing the peace,
      disrupting the law and order
      enforced by the heel of the city-state.

She declares, "I AM your God!"

The people cross
to the other side of the street
leaving Her unrecognized, abandoned.

After all,
what kind of God
would leave a temple of stone
and choose to live in flesh
when remaining in opulent isolation
would have been so much more
peaceful?

Third Sunday of Advent

"What then did you go out to see? Someone dressed in soft robes?
Look, those who wear soft robes are in royal palaces."
Matthew 11:8

Joy

The family
had approached the cashier
in fear and trembling,
anticipating the inevitability
of returning some items to the shelves.

A collective breath,
        to strengthen their hearts,
a murmuration of conversation as they decided
        who among them would be the one
        to nervously inquire about the balance
        on their card.

And oh, the blessed mother's face,
the moment it was revealed
that their benefits payment
had hit the account early.

Miracle! Bliss! Unspeakable joy!

Each one leapt to the shelves,
for indulgences like juice,
and bread, and milk.

But I was struck with a pang of sorrow
as I wondered what it would take
to crack open the vaults
of the elders and princes
and release the wealth of the nations
so that all the holy families
might finally witness the advent
of some truly good news.

Fourth Sunday of Advent

> In those days Mary set out and went with haste to a
> Judean town in the hill country... Luke 1:39

Love

In those days Elizabeth set out
and went with haste, for she had learned
that Mary was ready to deliver her baby.

She carried her infant, feet still tender
from her own time on the birth bricks.

She trusted that love would be the ointment
to ease the ache in her bones
as she set aside her own needs
to meet those of her kin.

From afar she could see the boundary,
rising up as an entreaty to the heavens,
its rough grey wall
casting shades of a toppled pillar of cloud.

She submitted to checkpoints,
to waiting in line, to limited hours of access.

She offered her documents
as paper sacrifices to an altar of bureaucracy.

She allowed her possessions to be scattered,
investigated, filtered, sorted.

She raised her child from her hip
so that her person might be inspected.

In the end, Mary labored alone,
with no doula to love her through her pains,
no baby cousin sleeping nearby.

And Elizabeth turned her face to the hills
and prayed that her kinswoman
would understand—

love was not absent, merely delayed
by The Barrier.

Christmas Eve/Nativity 1

But the angel said to them, "Do not be afraid; for see—I am
bringing you good news of great joy for all the people…"
Luke 2:10

The Longest Night

Grief at Christmas
is a string of lights
with one blown bulb.

An ornament
missing its string.

A carol sung
in discordant, minor key.

Beloveds,
be gentle with yourself,
and know:

Love
is here for you
too.

Christmas Day/Nativity 2

While they were there, the time came for her to deliver her child.
Luke 2:6

Governor

I had to practice saying his name: Quirinius.

And I got to wondering
as I sounded out the parts,
      as I spelled it out, signed it out,
      took a pen and underlined it out,

What was it about this man,
this unpopular, grasping, unfaithful,
      money-grubbing, bureaucratic,
      blood-soaked, despotic,
      representative-of-a-despised-empire,
what earned him this place in the natal tale?

I had to practice it.
So I could learn how
to pronounce it, to announce it,
to proclaim, defame, denounce it,
this name, this personification of the evils
besetting the people of God.

I needed to become deeply acquainted
so the whole congregation
could, with me, feel the gravitas of the moment
that it was then

when all hope was lost
and the worst of humanity
had been lifted up in leadership
over the faithful few

that it was
at
that
time

that liberation
was delivered.

Nativity 3

All things came into being through him, and without him not one thing came into being... John 1:3

Without Him

Ashley got the call, in late December.

We were just killing time, waiting
for the kids to arrive for after-school care
when her phone rang, and she answered
and got real serious.

It was snack time (crackers and cheese)
when she explained:
a baby, a Christmas Baby!

A case worker, searching for a provider
who could take in a child, short term,
probably just until New Year.

Over homework (spelling and long division)
it occurred to me to wonder:
would it not be easier to find a family
for a baby, a Noel Baby,
at Christmas than at other times?

"Oh no!" she shared,
(helping a child with his backpack
as his parents signed him out)
"It's much more difficult
at Christmas."

After all these years,
still no room, for the babe.

Later, as I wiped down tables,
I pondered those words
in the stillness of the empty room,

a room that mimicked a church
fallen strangely silent,
after all the promises made to Mary
when she went to the crisis pregnancy center
and was convinced to carry to term,

a room where children played
while we discussed a baby
and a mother
who would be forced to endure Christmas
without him.

First Sunday after Christmas

After three days they found him in the temple, sitting among the teachers, listening to them and asking them questions. Luke 2:46

In the Temple

I found Jesus.

I found them in the youth room,
their head lolling lazily
against the back of a black futon.

They had slipped away from their parents
for an hour of laughter, talk, and food.
They had stolen away
from the pressures of school
for an hour of learning.

I lost sight of them when we all stood
to move around the room
and I found myself dwarfed
by these sycamore trees.
And we swayed in the branches together
Jesus and me.

I found Jesus.

She was lying, face-down,
on a cast-off couch.
A combination of her meds and her ADHD
had robbed her of sleep, the previous night.

She had slipped away from her parents
for a nap.
She had stolen away
from the pressures of her peers
for half an hour in this hyperbaric chamber.

When the leader gave the instruction
to act out the story,
she gave an immense, deep sigh
and dragged herself from her cushion,
her sullen scowl at the others
a rebuke to the storm.
And we rode the waves together
Jesus and me.

I found Jesus.

He was running, full pelt, across the lawn
defiantly alive in a place of death.
He had slipped away from his parents
to wave his toddler arms
and shout at the clouds.

And as our mourning turned to laughter
he invited me to a deeper knowing
of the resilience of love.

And I understood myself to be:
not only listener but listing
          (leaning, more than learning)
not merely questioner but quester
          (the embodiment of a question).

And we inclined ourselves into the motion
of a swaying, spinning planet,
Jesus and me.

Holy Name of Jesus

So they shall put my name on the Israelites, and I will bless them.
Numbers 6:27

Consecration

In this moment
as you set aside
that which was yours in the past,
and take up
that which becomes yours today

Know that this action
is not a dishonoring of your yesterday,
for the joys and struggles of your history
are the particles of dust that form your core

Know that this action
is no panacea against the future,
for the coming days
will bring their moments to you,
no matter how you are called

Know that you are situated
at precisely the correct location
in the heavens,
placed among the constellations,
set in the skies for the fullness of this time
to be called by the name
that was intended to be yours
from before you were conceived.

As you receive this name as your own,
        your very own,
know that we receive you by this name,
        this very name
and we ask of the Universe
that all may know
that in the taking and keeping of this name
you are blessed.

New Year's Day

"And the king will answer them, 'Truly I tell you, just as you did it to one of the least of these who are members of my family, you did it to me.'" Matthew 25:40

Sodomite

They say, in the days following the feast,
that the Anti-Christ arrived:

surveying with scorn the hungry hordes,
snatching the baskets of leftovers
out of the hands of crying children,
saving the best for the wealthy
and requiring that the masses of the poor beg
and submit a urine sample
before the least of these could benefit
from literally the least that they could do.

They say, after the miracle,
that the Non-God appeared:

ushering the wealthy
into increasingly luxurious medical suites
with private beds and satellite TV,
while the poor waited in line for hours
at the free clinic and prayed
to whatever Divinity
there was left to believe in
that in the event of an unfortunate accident
they would not have
the unspeakable misfortune
of dying too slowly.

They say, on the heels of resurrection,
that the Un-Holy emerged:

oozing out of the cracks and crevices
to bring death instead of life,
to usher in the entrepreneur
and to reject the refugee,
to make public spectacles
of bathroom stalls and build up walls
instead of breaking down
the barriers that divide us.

They say, in the natal pangs of the new church,
that the Sodomite was born:

birthed into such an excess
of wealth and power
that a diversionary narrative was required
to hide the greed and cruelty
of their true nature
behind the mask of a false morality,
casting living human souls as villains
for demanding such indulgences as
privacy, human rights, and wedding cakes.

How could a people formed
in the image of a good and righteous God
ever bow before such tarnished thrones?

Second Sunday after Christmas

For God strengthens the bars of your gates and blesses your
children within you. Psalm 147:13

Live Nativity

When it's time
to put away the manger scene,
line the sheep up two-by-two,
place them in their cardboard ark,
as they prepare to take
their ten-month nap,

No need to leave feed in the trough.
The little lambs must do without,
despite the hunger they carried
from the farthest parts of the earth
to the innards of this crate.

When the day comes
to set aside the nativity set,
inspect each figurine for any chips and flaws
they may have gained on the journey,
throughout the hardships of this season,

Be sure to pull apart the holy family.
Corral them each into their own enclosures,
penalize the parents
with the absence of the child,
ensuring that a lonely wait in this pen
is their inheritance.

When the hour arrives
to dismantle the crèche,
wrap the babe in tissue paper,
in flimsy silver sheets
befitting a royal infant.

That will be adequate.
Consider the shining, shimmering
solar blanket
sufficient for this offspring of the stars,
enough to keep the baby warm
as the days in this cage are shivered away
until we decide to once again
make him known.

When the time comes
to leave Christmas behind,
how eagerly we pack the Child away.

Otherwise we could not continue to ignore
the reproachful gaze from painted eyes
as we deadlock the gates
of our sham Jerusalems,
and condemn the alien children
to a refuge of bars.

Epiphany

And having been warned in a dream not to return to Herod, they left for their own country by another road. Matthew 2:12

Homecoming

Balthazar was not pleased.
Her fingers gripped the steering wheel
as she pulled over to the side of the road,
"I'm telling you; the map is wrong!"

Melchior dropped his phone, exasperated,
"Two years of redirections
and recalculations,
as we avoided roadblocks and traffic stops,
and now you doubt the map?
This is where we started, our hometown,
does it look so different now
that you no longer have stars in your eyes?"

Caspar, in the back seat,
rolled down vis window,
"I don't see anything,
or anyone, I recognize."

The three sat and searched
for hints of the familiar,
among the organic food stores,
the coffee shops,
the suspiciously clean gutters,
and the signs declaring that loiterers
would be prosecuted.

Balthazar was not happy.
"This is not our home.
These are not our people.
Herod has made it here ahead of us
and brought in these changes."

She checked her side mirror
and pulled out into the flow of traffic,
and three penniless royals made their way
to another place, another town,
to search diligently
for somewhere to call home
on another road.

Baptism of Christ

The voice of the Sovereign One is over the waters; the God of
glory thunders, the Sovereign One, over mighty waters.
Psalm 29:3

Dyke

Yeah, you better fear me.

Fear me like you fear the embankment,
the levee near your home,
that creaks and groans as it prevents
the combined pressure of the weight
of all the rain in the world
from destroying all you hold dear.

Fear me because of all the power at my back
that I choose not to release.

Fear me in the scriptural sense.

Fear me because I am Miriam,
leading God's people in song
by the waters that swallowed Pharaoh;
because I am Deborah,
watching as the Kishon river
sweeps away my enemies;
because I am a million billion women
collecting water in the heat of the day
in defiance of your laws and labels.

Fear me in the biblical sense,
by which I mean to say—respect me.

Respect me as a woman,
as a being capable of indescribable strength
and compassion.

I have been set as a bow in the clouds,
I am the promise that walls off the divide
between life and death.

Test me and see what I can accomplish.
And remember, always remember,
to fear me.

Second Sunday after Epiphany

To each is given the manifestation of the Spirit for the common
good. 1 Corinthians 12:7

How to Love a Church

Wash your cup after coffee hour.

Greet a guest, join the choir,
teach the children.
Agree to serve on a committee.

Bring your talents, bring your energy,
bring your enthusiasm,
put your money in the plate,
show up for services,
show up.

Show up,
not because the doors are open
but because the invitation is open
to bring your whole self
to the gathering of selves
and dare to be challenged,
informed, inspired,
to be the one who challenges,
informs, inspires,
to be the presence that only you can bring
to the Beloved Community
in the tradition of the Spirit
of Love.

And love.
Do the hard stuff.
Stay in the room with the crying baby,
with the adult who glares at the crying baby,
with that person who gets on your last nerve.

Love the whole congregation,
stay in the conversation
even when you disagree,
especially when you disagree.
Stay because you disagree,

and leave
            because love can mean knowing
            when to wipe the dust and go
            when to say no.

And know within yourself
when you've been wrong,
when being strong feels more like bending,
like picking up the threads and mending,
like finding new instead of ending
and tending things you find surprising.

And find
to your surprise
that all the ways to love a church
are the same as all the ways to love yourself.

Greet a guest and show up,
be ready for the glow up,
you might even need to grow up,
proclaim your no, and sew up,
and wash
your own
damn
cup.

Third Sunday after Epiphany

As it is, there are many members, yet one body.
1 Corinthians 12:20

Autopsy

Go ahead, I will not disturb you.

Take your instruments to my Flesh
peel back the Skin, look inside.

Start here,
on the soft surface of my Thighs,
see where I have traced
the guidelines for you.
I did this thing in secret,
music turned up loud,
so my mother would not hear me crying,
as I engraved deep your hateful words.

I wonder, are there handprints?
I think perhaps you can still see the marks
of the hands that held me down
while my Clitoris was cut.
Such fear we have of a woman's desires.

Examine my neck,
notice the wound in my Throat,
just below my Adam's Apple.
I was sliced there when a stranger
took exception to my skirt;
as if the way a woman
chooses to clothe her body
is an invitation to violence.

Look now, to my Chin,
to the Skin around my Ears
see the skill of the surgeons.
They pulled me taut like a shroud
tugged my insides tight with self-hatred
tucked away the proof of my years.

I understand.
You did not expect to see it,
so much evidence of hatred
within this Frame.
So much of Me, melted,
by the acid of loathing.

You expected a bride,
I come to you, a corpse.

You have done this thing, I am eviscerated.

But come now, enough of talking.
You have a Body to tend to.

Fourth Sunday after Epiphany

If I speak in the tongues of mortals and of angels, but do not have
love, I am a noisy gong or a clanging cymbal. 1 Corinthians 13:1

Dogma

"You know me,"
you croon, softly, like a lover.
And you imagine your voice peals out,
clear as a bell,
drawing the faithful to worship.

"You know me!" you cry.
And it is the clamor of the claxon
that clears the factory floor
at the end of the shift,
releasing those who toil
not out of love but obligation.

You whimper, "You know me,"
as, with a hollow clang,
your last hope drops
like a bell from a burning steeple.

And I realize that I do know you.

I see you, no longer reflected dimly,
but face to face.

You name yourself Dogma,
but I name you False:
a libelous, pitiful ungod,
reflecting Divinity
only in the way that a mirror image
is directly opposite of the true form.

Released from your clinging hold,
I rush to the embrace of Mystery,
to the wonder of Uncertainty,
to the great, eternal, holy beauty,
            of the Unknown.

Presentation of Christ

"...and a sword will pierce your own soul too." Luke 2:35

Mary Mourns

You never actually lose someone.

They sneak up on you
at the most inconvenient times
and lean over your shoulder,
so real you could introduce them
to the server pouring your drink.

You don't lose them, they leave you.

They slip away in the still hours of the night,
they vanish when your back is turned,
or they're taken away before your eyes,
forcibly evicted from life.

And you're left
with the shape of their absence,
forensic evidence of their presence:
a note written in their own hand,
glasses, still smudged with their fingerprints.

And when these signs go unnoticed
you grab the world by the shoulders
and shake it, offended, by the audacity
of a planet continuing to turn without them.

Next thing you know, you're Simeon,
making the unknown known in the holy places:
"Here is the one, my revelation,
my glorious all."

Their name is a prayer on your lips,
a sacrifice of suffering,
but you embrace the pain of it,
this tax you pay for it,
clutching love's shadow to your chest,
embedding it into your soul
because you know the truth of it,

the thing that kills you is not
the sting of the blade as it enters,
it's the vacancy that remains when it's gone.

Fifth Sunday after Epiphany

Then one of the seraphs flew to me, holding a live coal that had
been taken from the altar with a pair of tongs. Isaiah 6:6

Virago

It is fair to say
that I did not meet the prophet
on my best day
but it was certainly my loudest.

I took to the streets, I was not taken.
I took to speaking, I was not silenced.

I had fled from their condemnation
wearing only tattered shreds of my dignity.

I made my accusation in the marketplace,
Unapologetic.

I named them all that day.

I opened my mouth and discovered
my tongue burned clean by a holy coal.

I used words I had not known I knew
I blistered the air and their ears.

I made my case to the dust
to the dirt that the prophets of old
once wore to challenge the kings
in the courts of power.

And so, it was
that only I witnessed
what the great teacher inscribed
with his finger on the ground.

I did not hear what was said.
I did not see them turn and leave.
I remained there, awestruck
gazing at the inscription
until a dropped rock
rolled over it.

And then I looked for the first time
into the face of the one who remained
whose eyes were red-rimmed as mine
whose mouth trembled
with grief, and distaste, and rage
just like mine.

The dust of the road still swirled
from the displacement of the last feet
to beat a hasty retreat
as we gazed at each other, face to face

And I saw the soul
of the one who had written,
"Me too."

Sixth Sunday after Epiphany

"Woe to you when all speak well of you, for that is what their
ancestors did to the false prophets." Luke 6:26

Plain Speaking

My whiteness is a sheet.
I pull it up to my chin
to hide beneath the fiction of vulnerability,
when in truth I know myself to be
not so far removed from robe-clad,
torch-bearing cowards.

Woe to me, for I have been cowardly.

My whiteness is a mask.
I hold it before my face
to hide behind the fiction of solidarity,
when in all honesty my first instinct—
when push comes to shove—
is to look out for myself.

Woe to me, for I have been selfish.

My whiteness is a book.
I poke my nose in it
to hide within the fictions of the past,
when in reality I write these pages myself
when I refuse to challenge history's lies.

Woe to me, for I have been a liar.

What a comical epiphany,
to bask in the warm beam of sunlight
as it streams through the stained-glass face
of White Jesus
and to realize his story is told
in a text which contains
no white characters.

Woe to me, for I have been obtuse.

Do not speak well of me
for finally grasping this revelation.

Better that I be reviled
for too long accepting
the dogma of false prophets
who have done their utmost
to fade, to bleach, to sanitize
the good news of a brown-skinned,
itinerant, activist, radical
whose message is anything
but white.

Seventh Sunday after Epiphany

"But I say to you that listen, Love your enemies, do good to those
who hate you…" Luke 6:27

Pyrite

Ok, but I told him this was terrible advice.

And he was all, "Oh Martha,
the people are smart enough to realize
this is a message for a movement,
it's a call to community,
it's a proclamation to the powerful
that my realm is made of different stuff
than the kingdoms of this world."

Hashtag: Not All Kingdoms.

If he'd listened, I could've told him
the people are definitely not smart enough.

And now this message for a movement
has been distilled to poison for the powerless,
a toxin prescribed from the pulpit
for the vulnerable in the pews
who share their beds with their enemies
and serve breakfast to their abusers
who turn bruised cheeks for raised fists
and who pray and pray and pray
and stay

in homes where love is absent.

Transfiguration Sunday

And while Jesus was praying, the appearance of his face changed,
and his clothes became dazzling white. Luke 9:29

Danny

It took a while
before he could screw up the nerve
to do the injections himself.

Some might say,
that's when the miracle happened.

As if the changes to his clothing,
to the shape of his face,
to his hard-won legally recognized name
were the markers that made him a man.

I would say the marvel was found
in those who had faith,
the ones who did not require
a voice from the heavens declaring
"This is my Son, my Chosen; listen to him!"

In truth, he is who he has always been.
It is only ever the world's perception of him
that required transformation.

Ash Wednesday

Blow the trumpet in Zion; sanctify a fast; call a solemn
assembly...Joel 2:15

Gaia

Gather the elders from the rooftops,
    from the high places
    where they have sought refuge
    from the roaring trumpet winds,
    as nature rages
    against our corruption,
summon the elders to the assembly.

Collect the families from the ground,
    from earth that quakes
    in the absence of God,
    from fields that shiver
    and crack open with a terrible sigh
    to release ancient pockets
    of toxic gas, poisoning the air,
    setting fire to water,
    as creation reels from our violence,
summon the families to the assembly.

Pluck the children from the flames,
    from the beaches where they shelter
    where they swelter and sweat
    in the noon-day darkness
    as clouds of ash turn day to night,
    and trees explode from infernos
    of our own making,
summon the children to the assembly.

Call the people from the coastline
        from waters that do not spring up
        so much as seep up,
        from oceans that nibble
        at the edges of the shore
        as glaciers weep
        at our catastrophic greed,
call the people to the assembly.

Let the meeting of nations be called to order.
Perhaps, even now, if we act
we may be spared.

First Sunday in Lent

Jesus, full of the Holy Spirit, returned from the Jordan and was
led by the Spirit in the wilderness... Luke 4:1

Follow

Hah!
He had a terrible sense of direction.
He never could manage to go
directly from point alpha to beta.

Once, when we reached a crossroads,
Simon walked on ahead
in an attempt to keep us on track
but the Nazarene said,
"I'm the leader here, get behind me."

And of course
there's the time he, famously,
got himself lost, alone, in the desert
and wandered aimlessly
for what must have seemed like days.

We wondered how long it would have taken
for him to find his own way out.
Thomas said he doubted forty years
would be long enough.
And the Nazarene grumbled in reply,
"Don't tempt me to go back to the desert."

Honestly, he had all the local knowledge
of a tourist.

I mean.
Who, having ever studied a map,
would travel from Gennesaret
to Bethsaida via Tyre?

And yet, when I think back it strikes me
that no matter how far he led us
from the usual path,
he had a knack for ending up
right where he was needed most.

And that is something worth emulating.

Second Sunday in Lent

Just then a man from the crowd shouted, "Teacher, I beg you to
look at my son; he is my only child." Luke 9:38

Supplication

How tightly wound you are, my child,
bound by this shame within you.

Your jaw clenches, your muscles tense,
your words collect behind a face
stretched taut from the tension
of maintaining the expected smile.

How desperately
you fight against the strength
of the monster inside
that would burn out the pain with flame,
drown out the noise with water,
cut out the cancer with blades,
pelt the enemy into submission
with pills.

Well.
I will pray the shame away.

I will keep you safe until the One comes
who will recognize you
as another soul in need of transfiguration.

My child,
while you bite your tongue
against the words that would free you
my own mouth will move
like a babbling brook,
unceasing in supplications
to the Compassionate One;

prayers that you will be brought out
in the coming out,
until the whole world is dazzled
by the sparkle in your eyes
giving testimony to the unquenchable flame
of your fabulous soul.

Third Sunday in Lent

At that very time there were some present who told him about the
Galileans whose blood Pilate had mingled with their sacrifices.
Luke 13:1

Amends

Sunday, 2008, Knoxville
as church youth prepare to perform.
Shots fired.

Monday, 2007, Blacksburg
as budding scholars wake for class.
Shots fired.

Tuesday, 1999, Columbine
as hungry students pause for lunch.
Shots fired.

Wednesday, 2018, Parkland
as bored teens watch the clock.
Shots fired.

Thursday, 2015, Charleston
as faithful members pause for prayer.
Shots fired.

Friday, 2012, Newtown
as little children learn their letters.
Shots fired.

Saturday, 2016, Orlando
as Latine queers order last-call drinks.
Shots fired.

Each day of the week, every year, any place

we mingle their sacrificial blood
on pews, in dorms, over books,
along halls, in bathrooms, on dance floors

as lawmakers wash their hands in blood
and dry them on the Constitution.
Shots fired.

And unless we repent, we all will perish.

Annunciation of Christ

Then Mary said, "Here am I, the servant of the Lord; let it be with
me according to your word." Then the angel departed from her.
Luke 1:38

Homo

I guess the angel was late,
stuck on the tarmac, slow to take flight:
missed the meeting with Mary.

So, she never got the message
that this *homoousios* child was
holy, sacred, blessed of God.
And she never uttered the words,
(my paraphrase)
"I will accept you as you are."

Maybe the angel was drunk,
bottle in hand, passed out in a bar:
junked the job with Joseph.

So, he never got the message
that this *homoousios* child was
precious, rare, blessed of God.
And he never spoke the words,
(unrecorded, but inferred)
"I will claim you as my own."

Perhaps the angel got lost,
took a wrong turn, GPS signal missing:
couldn't connect with the couple.

So, they never got the message
that this *homoousios* child was
fragile, threatened, blessed of God.
And they never made the oath
(as implied by actions)
"We will protect you at any cost."

How else can we even begin to understand?

When Herod's soldiers came,
and the hills echoed
with the anguished shouts of the fathers
and the trees trembled
at the keening wails of the mothers,
When the crunch came, when the crisis came,
when love had never mattered more,

What other explanation could there be,
for the decision they made?

How else could they give over
the flesh and bone, heart and soul,
life and limb
of this *homoousios* child
to death's rough arms?

I guess ... maybe ... perhaps ...
the angel never came, so
the child was cast into the streets.

Fourth Sunday in Lent

On the day after the passover, on that very day, they ate the
produce of the land, unleavened cakes and parched grain.
Joshua 5:11

Food Desert

Mrs. Lot wanted vegetables for her children
to nourish them on life's journey.
But there was nowhere to buy fresh produce
since her local grocery shut its doors.
So she turned to the dollar store for food,
and her family became pillars of salt.

Jacob was delighted when his sons returned
with the news of Joseph's invitation.
But the transmission went out on their car,
so they walked to the mini mart
for cans of spiced ham
instead of feasting on the fat of the land.

Martha thought she might grow corn
in the garden behind her apartment.
But the land was sold to a big-box store
and planted with crops of warehouses.
So the only grain to harvest on the Sabbath
was a package of gas station snack cakes.

Philip wished he had the resources
to feed all his hungry students.
But it was too expensive to throw a feast
with food from the convenience store.
So, the class had to snack on crackers
instead of loaves and fish.

And so it goes in the promised land
where the wealthy live on milk and honey
and do their best to ignore the people of God
starving in the desert
since the manna ran out.

Fifth Sunday in Lent

I am about to do a new thing; now it springs forth, do you not perceive it? I will make a way in the wilderness and rivers in the desert. Isaiah 43:19

Former Things

When she left, it was in a hurry,
in a panic, in a flurry of fear.
When she left, she fled,
down an unlit path.

When she left, she abandoned
a houseful of things
and decades of memories.
When she left, she took
what was needed, required, essential
and let slip the things that were not.

When she left, it was a stepping out
into the wilderness.

When the obscenity
of rage-fueled words
violated the day,
when the violence
of fist meeting flesh
tainted the night,
she huddled with her children
and in holy whispers declared
"Enough!"

When she left,
she threw herself with wild abandon
into the tempestuous depths
of the fathomless unknown
and discovered
sanctuary.

Liturgy of the Palms

After he had said this, he went on ahead, going up to Jerusalem.
Luke 19:28

Subversive

He was still picking his teeth clean
from the meal with Zacchaeus,
when he told the tale of the Anti-Christ:
the nobleman deeply disliked
who purchased his way into power,
who bullied his servants into usury,
and slaughtered his opponents.

He was still exhaling the words
when he showed them, by example,
what noble really means:
the peasant leader wildly loved
who borrowed his seat into the city,
who asked his friends to follow freely,
on the way to meet his own death
at the hands of his enemies.

He was still within the chaos of the crowd
when he wept for peace,
still wiping the tears from his cheeks
when he raged at the robbers.

He was still, emphatically,
the antithesis of empire
with every word and action
until the very end.

And still they ask the church
not to get political.

Liturgy of the Passion

Then one of them struck the slave of the high priest and cut off his
right ear. Luke 22:50

In the Line of Duty

The funny thing about that night,
thinking back,
is that right up until the moment it happened
I was complaining
about how cold my ears were.

Even now there is a numbness,
defying the skill of the healer's hands,
a reminder of the wound.
       Nothing, of course,
       compared to the mental scars
       that violence always leaves behind.

My buddies tell me that
when the blow struck
I just stood there, dazed,
for the longest time
before crumpling down into a heap
on the ground.

Seems accurate.
I've been down here ever since.
Well I tried, I have tried, to rise.
It turns out that regular, normal, civil,
civilian life
is the harder fight to face.

But a house is no place
for a soldier's frontline.

So to save my family
from the friendly fire of my inner battles
I make my home in the streets
and warm myself by a campfire
that hints at the promise of life.

Monday of Holy Week

Six days before the Passover Jesus came to Bethany, the home of
Lazarus, whom he had raised from the dead. John 12:1

Bandages

The stench of death
was heavy over the place.
The servants fled from the smell
of rotting flesh.
By the second week
we gave my brother up for dead.

They came in off the road,
rowdy and dirt-stained,
this *mamzer* and his friends.

An unfortunate time to be seeking welcome.

"Why have you come?" I demanded,
"My brother dies!"

He clapped a weathered hand
to the shoulders of his friends.
"Go take your rest," he told them,
"I have work to do here."

Four days he labored
bathing frail limbs,
applying and reapplying
strips of linen to festering wounds.

Four days in that tomb of a room
before Lazarus,
with a mighty gasp,
clutched at his chest and asked,
astonished, who had removed the stone.

And the Nazarene with tears trailing
through the dust on his cheeks,
and glistening in his beard,
with an open-mouthed grin
proclaimed: "Your brother lives!"

Tuesday of Holy Week

I have been like a portent to many, but you are my strong refuge.
Psalm 71:7

Freak

After leaving the court,
the shouts of the people
ringing through the halls,
my feet drag, and I linger,
resisting what is to come.

I have walked in the halls of men
celebrated, embraced, accepted.
I have railed against this physical cage.
I have lived beyond the limits of my skin.
I have refused to be defined by this flesh.

Rough hands grasp at clinging cloth
(fabric parts reluctantly from sweaty skin)
pooling on the ground
with the hiss of a snake,
the hiss of in-drawn breath.

It has come down to this:
a profane disrobing,
the fullness of who I Am
diminished to the false evidence
of this small frame.

I think: their revulsion hurts more
than their fists will.
Then the blows begin
and I understand, intimately,
the misery of the vulnerable
in this holistic reality of pain.

Their hatred steals their humanity.
They appear before me as ghouls, demons,
freaks.

My God, my God, why have you forsaken me
to the monsters that lurk
between the benches and lockers
of this high school changing room?

Wednesday of Holy Week

After saying this Jesus was troubled in spirit, and declared, "Very truly, I tell you, one of you will betray me." John 13:21

Fingers

Xanthippe,
my new neighbor,
tells me she heard
he was sold out for cash.

But I can tell you this:
the only pieces of silver I know of
were the ones tied securely
beneath my skirts
as I bustled through the streets
hoping to post bail
for the Nazarene.

They turned me away.

And now that our stories
are being pinned on a page
it troubles me to think that our people
          his own people
are being cast as scapegoats
for the cruelty of empire.

It seems a little too neat, to me,
that all those fingers
have started pointing back
at us lot.

Well I tell you,
I saw the smirk on the face of the guards
when I asked for him by name.

I know where my finger points.

Maundy Thursday

For as often as you eat this bread and drink this cup, you proclaim the Lord's death until he comes. 1 Corinthians 11:26

Meal

They always leave out the part,
right there between the wine and the walk,
when he turned to me and said, "Martha,
don't let them make a fuss about this."

For the first few years
I assumed he was talking about the arrest,
and all that followed.

But now, while this group argues
over the type of bread
and that group fights
over juice or wine
I remember that when he spoke
he did so through his last bite of food.

"Don't let them make a fuss."

It was as if he knew
the flights of fancy that would follow,
knew that someone hard-headed, efficient,
and down-to-earth
would be needed to tell them all:

"This bread and this wine"

simply the common everyday fare
that sits before us every time we eat.
This invitation to bring him to mind
at every meal, with each bite and sip:

it was never meant to cause
such indigestion.

Good Friday

...Meanwhile, standing near the cross of Jesus were his mother,
and his mother's sister, Mary the wife of Clopas, and Mary
Magdalene. John 19:25

Last Gasp

You would think all Israel had been there
the way people go on about it.

My cousin's aunt's neighbor
loves to brag about being in the crowd
and pushing to the front
for her own special blessing
       and I know for a fact
       she has never traveled further
       than half a day's walk
       from Nain.

There's all kinds of talk
about what he said or didn't say
or sang or didn't sing,
as if he could do anything more
than beg for breath,
and for his mama.

But we who were truly present
will never forget her voice.

You haven't known pain
until you've witnessed
the wide-mouthed scream
of a mother
whose child has been murdered
      by an unjust state,
      by authorities who require
      that she crowd-fund and beg
      until she can afford
      to bury the body.

That pain
is breathtaking.

Holy Saturday

*Oh that you would hide me in Sheol, that you would conceal me
until your wrath is past, that you would appoint me a set time, and
remember me! Job 14:13*

Saturday

"Let's skip this day,"
Mary said, when I woke her.

I admit the heaviness of the house
inclined me to feel that the living room
had never been so poorly named.

James growled at John,
and they both slouched from the room,
returning to their nets.

Lazarus curled in the corner,
clutching a copy of his own bail bond
to his chest as he slept.

Judas called for water, his face still swollen
from the soldiers' beating
the night before.

Simon stumbled up the stairs,
back from wherever he'd got to.
His eyes could not meet mine
as he dropped a dead rooster on the counter
and turned again to go.

That day lasted for a week,
the sun too lazy to move.
The shades of the walls grew and stretched
and met in the middle of the room,
touching on the scattered remains
of Thursday's supper.

My stomach said, "I hunger."

I made a meal of crusts,
the remnants of a feast.
And there, alone, I remembered.

Easter Vigil

But on the first day of the week, at early dawn, they came to the tomb, taking the spices that they had prepared. Luke 24:1

Incompatible

At Epiphany
you lay down gifts with the Magi,
professions of faith
in the widening of Mystery.
You say: this is love.
But when Mary comes out at the altar
you are infuriated.

In Sunday School
you teach of the covenant between men
that predates the vows with Michal
You say: this is love.
But when David shares that he, also,
is drawn to two or more genders,
you become afraid.

At the Valentine's supper
you revere the romancing of Rachel
as proof of the power of persistence.
You say: this is love.
But when Leah asks
to be seated with both her Beloveds,
she is made to suffer.

At Easter
you fetishize the flagellation of flesh,
thrilling at the lash of the whip.
You say: this is love.
But when Simon admits
to a fondness for spanking,
ze is compelled to leave.

At Pentecost
you exult the tale of the Ethiopian
and exalt the Divine One who welcomes all.
You say: this is love.
But when Philip shares their pronouns
they are prevented from baptism.

We are vessels of clay,
each filled with our own motley mix
of aromatic spices,
denied access to the tomb.

You hand us a text, and we find our faces
in the wild diversity of tales
contained within this queer book
We say: this is love.

But you yank the leash
on your adamantine-chained,
three-headed God
and decide for yourselves what is good.

How can the contradictions
between your message of life
and your ministry of death
ever be made
compatible?

Resurrection of Christ

Early on the first day of the week, while it was still dark, Mary
Magdalene came to the tomb and saw that the stone had been
removed from the tomb. John 20:1

Breath

The stench of death
was heavy over the place.

We came in off the road,
cowed and tear-stained,
this *mamzer*'s faithful friends.

An unfortunate time
to be out of the house
so early—and yet days late—
burdened with strips of linen
and herbs to medic fatal wounds.

It was a mundane miracle
to be in that place of death
still slightly out of breath from the walk
the evidence of life
puffing from our mouths.

I confess I was astonished.
Who had removed the stone?

And the Nazarene,
that weighty corpse that had flopped
so convincingly to the dust,
where was he?

My sister was ready to raise a ruckus.
Her lips began to murmur
"What do we do, what do we do,
what-do-we-do?"

I touched her sleeve, gently, "Mary."
We looked at each other
and spoke no more.

It was enough.

Easter Evening

And he said to them, "What are you discussing with each other while you walk along?" They stood still, looking sad. Luke 24:17

Feet

He slipped, you know,
on all that oil.

The men laughed when he rose unsteadily,
sliding on her perfumed gift.
Then his feet flew out from beneath him
and his backside hit the stone floor.

I hid my chuckle in my hands.

He was kind—of course!
He defended her when his friends got mad.

I suppose the washing was fine
and this business with the hair was,
well.

I would have fetched her a towel
had she asked.

But the oil…

Oh, how he lamented the next night
when a day of action on softened feet
resulted in a fresh sheet of blisters.

Poor girl, she wasn't to know.
He needed them tough for walking.

Second Sunday of Easter

But Peter and the apostles answered, "We must obey God rather than any human authority." Acts 5:29

Another Scroll

The task of the faithful remains this:

On those days
when the tyrant has toasted his toes
over the smoldering remains of papyrus
smudged with your own sweat and tears
and sent your amanuensis
scrambling back to your side,
bearing news of Jehoiakim's pride—
On those days, take another scroll.

In those years,
when steel-clad conquistadors
have crushed the muscles and bones
of the enslaved with parchments
emblazoned with official seals,
and sent disease and famine
among the people,
bearing death and calling it life…
In those years, take another scroll.

In those times,
When the Leader has legislated loathing
and legitimized the loathsome
with military uniforms,
and prescribed papers and stars
and death squads and trains
bearing the bodies to the End of the line…
In those times, take another scroll.

On these days,
When the Puppet is plumping his pillow
in golden chambers
built on the backs of unpaid bills,
where he tweets in the small hours
to stir new flames from coals of hatred,
to warm Stromboli's bed
while Geppetto weeps
in blood-soaked streets...
On this day, take another scroll.

Third Sunday of Easter

He said to them, "Cast the net to the right side of the boat, and you will find some." So they cast it, and now they were not able to haul it in because there were so many fish. John 21:6

Missed Catch

Oh, you latter scribes
who write in the Pauline tradition,
what little marks you make
as you write to me with your own hand!

How few are your pages!
How small, your words!

And yet
you have become the "well, actually"
of every devil's advocate
of every squashing thumb.

Your arbitrary proscriptions
are a thorn in our flesh,
your rules, a bait and switch
of the freedom we have been offered.

You have cast a net of shame
from the wrong side of the boat
and you wonder why we slip away.
Take note: I have had my fill of you.

Gently, and with love, I rebuke you.
I have heard your argument and I offer,
by way of reply, the fullness, the depth and breadth and width,
of the revelation of all that is holy.

In short, I throw the book at you.

Fourth Sunday of Easter

Jesus answered, "I have told you, and you do not believe. The
works that I do in my Father's name testify to me..." John 10:25

Miracle

Yes, I saw my share of miracles.

They are not, perhaps, as thrilling
as others you have read about.

But, marvel at this:
once, at the end of a long day,
we gathered with aching feet
and empty stomachs
and He said, "Well, what's to eat?"

So Philip baked bread
and we each shared a little left from lunch,
so that we might continue to enjoy
each other's company.

Wonder at this:
one day as we all tried to enter
a home in Capernaum
we found the doorway too narrow
to allow us to usher through
the followers who were
paralyzed, or older, or injured.
He said, "Well, what now?"

But the homeowners,
willingly swung the hammers
to knock out the door frame
so that we might all be able to meet together.

Consider this revelation:
on one of our regular commutes
to the more dangerous side of the lake,
a storm of disagreement broke out among us
as some disciples tallied up
how much of our meager budget
was being spent on Others.
He said, "Well, and why not?"

And a great calm spread across us
as we each recalculated
our definition of kin.

Maybe my legends are too little
to register as miracles;
but for me,
as I pass my days in a hostile world
that wants nothing more than to
divide the weakest from the pack
and devour us whole,
I hold onto these tales as precious portents
of a community worth building.

Fifth Sunday of Easter

Then I saw a new heaven and a new earth; for the first heaven and
the first earth had passed away, and the sea was no more.
Revelation 21:1

Pangaea

And just like that, it was over.

We awoke to find
that every ocean, river, and stream
(those barriers that for too long defined us)
had been tamed and sent below,
and the continents
(those great heaving masses of arbitrary dirt)
were subsumed into geographical unity.

We quenched our thirst
with water from deep wells,
and surveyed the freshly revealed landscape.

On that day there were no borders,
no nation constructs,
no fictions of fealty to a flag.

There was no longer any impediment
to the movement of the people
as they passed from Pharaoh to freedom.

So it became in all our best interests
to ensure that no part of this new Pangaea
could boast of any greater wealth or liberty
than the rest.

Then at last Alan Kurdi
and Angie Valeria
sprang forth from their water-logged caskets
and danced, laughing, in the sand.

Sixth Sunday of Easter

Jesus said to him, "Stand up, take your mat and walk." John 5:8

Throne

My father forgot about
my mother's fear of heights
the day he helpfully moved her
so close to the edge
of the Rundle Mall glass elevator
that her knees pressed into the panes.

He had yet to learn
that she would choose the placement
of her own body.

He was not the last to misunderstand.

At the marketplace
people politely averted their gaze,
missing the miracle of mobility
as she took up her wheels and went.

> In later days,
> we would be ushered in
> to the holy of holies,
> the seconds of sacred silence
> as we awaited the angel of death.

Yet, there remains this theophany:

Mum, reigning from her wheeled throne,
sharp turns sending sparks,
igniting into flames at her sides,
silver-streaked hair
streaming in her wake:

Divinity, set loose upon the world.

Ascension of Christ

When he had said this, as they were watching, he was lifted up,
and a cloud took him out of their sight. Acts 1:9

Do

Every now and then
(less so, now that my knees ache)

I stroll up to that hilltop
broom in hand
and shoo away another group
of cloud-gazers.

I tell them, as I'm telling you:

"The tomb was empty!
So, what of it?

Go and grab some bandages,
there are still wounds
that need tending!

Get into trouble,
the good kind of trouble,
even when it sets you against your own kin.

Get up and go and
breathe
in the face of hell
so that no one can deny
your proof of life.

But don't lay around here all day
looking up at the sky
there's just too much to do!"

Seventh Sunday of Easter

But when her owners saw that their hope of making money was
gone, they seized Paul and Silas and dragged them into the
marketplace before the authorities. Acts 16:19

Cleaning House

I wonder
if the real reason he got so angry
at the money changers in the temple
was not only due to the defiling of that house
but the debasing of all the homes
yet to come.

I wonder if those few tables
kaleidoscoped in glittering horror,
if he had a vision of endless iterations
of this profanation
of the purchasing of souls.

I wonder
if he caught a glimpse of humanity
sold like cattle in the marketplace,
of black sacrosanct skin
ripped apart by the master's whip,

of hoop-skirted doves, willfully ignorant
and cheerfully complicit,
sipping tea on the porches
of whitewashed tombs,

of temples consecrated to coin,
rising above fields fertilized
with sacrificial blood
and planted with the bones of the dead.

It is no wonder
that the one who came
for the least and the lost
came a little unglued in the presence
of those with the most
profiting from the sweat of the rest
in the house of the First and the Last.

Visitation of Mary to Elizabeth

> Rejoice with those who rejoice, weep with those who weep.
> Romans 12:15

Cousins

Was Elizabeth jealous
of Mary's good fortune
in having her son returned to her?

Did she regret the hours spent
gently shushing into Mary's ear
over that long weekend?

> Three days of sorrow,
> a late payment
> for three months of joy
> in the hill country.

Did she struggle to rejoice with her kin
as they stood before the open tomb,
when the fruit of her own womb
did not leap so freely back to life?

Or did she do what mourning mothers do?

Did she gather up what remained of him,
his cast-off clothes,
his favorite story,
the memory of his laughter,
and offer them in love
for life?

Perhaps she did
a little bit
of both.

Day of Pentecost

Divided tongues, as of fire, appeared among them, and a tongue rested on each of them. Acts 2:3

Riot

Who set these streets on fire?

It blew up from the embers
of the coals in the courtyard
where empire warmed itself
while it made false accusations,
against one whose cheek
was kissed with melanin.

It smoldered in our midst
until we could deny him no more,

It blazed with righteous indignation
until tongues of flame danced
above all our heads.

And ash filled the sky,
and tears filled our eyes.
We gasped in like a bellows,
blew out with a shout
giving voice to the rage
in an almighty babble,
and we took to the streets
as an ungoverned rabble.
We screamed, "Say his name!"
in the face of the devil,
with a fury that matched

to the scope of the evil
of an empire that kills
with a smirk and a shrug,
takes an innocent life
and calls him a thug.
Yes, we took to the streets
in the Spirit of love.

Pentecost is a riot.

Beloveds, get ready,
the flames are licking at the door.

Trinity Sunday

… what are human beings that you are mindful of them, mortals
that you care for them? Psalm 8:4

Family Night

They sit on the steps
of the Red Door Church,
And make their plans for the evening
a night on the town in Saint Louis

They'll have to split up.
The beds for women are all taken.
Son wishes Mother and Sister well
and goes to find a place to lay his head,
while the women sit there, reminiscing.

Mother remembers a time
before he grew so tall, his beard so long.
They recall the way
his presence opened doors.

Oh, how those once-tiny feet
would lead them beside the waters
of hot soapy showers
and flushing toilets.
How the rise and fall
of his little chest in breathing
warmed even the hardest of hearts.

The feet are grown now and hardened.
The only notice of his breath
is the face people make
at the decaying of his teeth.
It has been many a winter
since people stopped to marvel
at the babe.

Now he is a man, a troublesome man,
a challenging, difficult, uncomfortable man.
Now no one wants Mother,
and Sister's spirit is all burnt out.
So, they split up—
and no one is there to witness the obscenity
of separating One into Many,
of dividing community into disunity.

Thus in the doorway of the church,
the divine creator of the universe
rests her head on the stone steps
and weeps for a world that has no room
for a Holy God, brought low.

Proper 7/12

There is no longer Jew or Greek, there is no longer slave or free,
there is no longer male and female; for all of you are one in Christ
Jesus. Galatians 3:28

One

Before the Battle of the Sexes,
before Eve lamented or Adam toiled,
before the serpent
played man against woman,
before the parts were forcefully excised
from the whole:
the first human inhabited flesh.

Observe the integrity of their naked body,
bear witness to them in their fullness,
still damp from the clay,
lovingly made in the whole image of God.

Is this why Mary sang
that her soul magnified
and her spirit rejoiced?

Perhaps she understood that this new *adam*,
setting sacred, genderqueer feet upon our *adamah*,
would engender life for all genders
would, by Their very existence,
embody the reconciliation
of all that had been torn asunder.

Behold: They who make us One.

Discover in Them the assurance that—
       beyond the arbitrary designations
       of feminine or masculine,
       behind the labels and libels
       of 'butch' or 'sissy'—
you are as you are, fully human,
complete and whole.

Proper 8/13

By contrast, the fruit of the Spirit is love, joy, peace, patience,
kindness, generosity, faithfulness, gentleness, and self-control.
There is no law against such things. Galatians 5:22–23

Husband

I made myself small for you.
I took it all—the taunting,
the vitriol, the manipulation.
I absorbed your anger so the world
would only see your strength.

I subjected myself to you.
I submitted to the ropes
of your domesticity.
I wove my own hair
into the fabric of our bed
the better to serve your needs.

My hair is shorn now, seven locks gone.
I have named them:
this one is Joy, that one Patience
here is Kindness and Goodness
these two are Faithfulness and Gentleness.
This one—the most stubborn—
I have named it Self-Control.

You thought the sound
was the clicking of scissors, but no:
it was the soft metallic *snick*,
seven times, of seven locks springing open.

You have painted me in public
as your Delilah,
but, husband, this was your own doing.
It was you who strained against
the two pillars of Love and Peace;
it was you who brought the house down.
A fitting end, for an ungodly marriage.

Proper 9/14

As a mother comforts her child, so I will comfort you; you shall be
comforted in Jerusalem. Isaiah 66:13

Mother's Lament

Allow me to introduce them,
these blessed ones: my daughters.

My Hagar suckles the master's son
while her own Ishmael withers
in the indifferent shade of the sugar cane.

Bathsheba bears the sons
of the warlord who raped her
and killed her husband.

Young Mary rocks her infant
with arms better suited
to bearing schoolbooks than a baby.

How many births
did my nameless daughter endure
in the quest to give Jesse his sons?

And where is the salvation
for my beloved, bold Anna,
cast into Simeon's shadow?

Cold comfort, to these,
that they might be saved
through childbearing.

Tuck the memory of all my daughters
into my soil, into my care, into their bed.
They have no need of men's fiefdoms;
their Mother has them now.

Proper 10/15

All the paths of the Lord are steadfast love and faithfulness, for those who keep God's covenant and decrees. Psalm 25:10

Plumb Line

Legend says
these pews were once ragged and raw,
hewn whole from Abraham's oak.
Today, their smoothness is a testament
to those of us who have been here since,
subsuming the splinters with our skin.

Legend says
this paten was pulled from the earth
the molten mess cast into a slab.
Today, its shine is a testament
to the salt from our shame-scorched cheeks
that buffed this brass plate to a mirror finish.

Legend says
this text was once a pile of stone
dragged from the base of Mount Sinai.
Today, the leaves are a testament
to the pulp of our spirits, pounded and dried
and pressed between the book covers.

Legend says
this church was founded on rock.
Today your pulpit flounders in sand.
We hold a plumb line as a testament
against the twists of your path.

Proper 11/16

But Martha was distracted by her many tasks; so she came to him and asked, "Lord, do you not care that my sister has left me to do all the work by myself? Tell her then to help me." Luke 10:40

Broom

We have so few domestic tales
that touch upon the lives of women,
so just in case anyone is inclined
to weaponize this one:

There were no gaping mouths,
no hushed whispers, no judging gazes;
men did not faint, Mary did not cry,
I did not nag.

The simple sequence of events was this:

I welcomed him
and his friends, and their dust,
into my clean home
and when I saw the mess they had made...

I handed him a broom.

Proper 12/17

> When the Sovereign One first spoke through Hosea, the
> Sovereign One said to Hosea, "Go, take for yourself a wife of
> whoredom..." Hosea 1:2

Gomer's Complaint

"Come as you are," the preacher said,
"Just as you are, no need to change."

So, I stood,
and excuse-me'd my way
along the narrow row towards the aisle
and as I went my shoes caught
on someone's feet, tripping me,
so, I left them behind.

"Come as you are."
So I swayed down the aisle,
hands reaching out to steady me,
and cloaking me with loose linen garments.

"Come as you are," the singer crooned.
So I elbowed my way through the crowd
and the piercings in my face
snagged in their hair,
plucked from my flesh.

"Come as you are,"
scrolled across the screen,
but the altar was too high from the ground.

So, I reached into my heart
and plucked out my hopes and dreams,
all the lost loves and yearnings,
I cracked open my skull
and dragged out my brains,
every hard-won belief,
every memory of joy and life,
and I piled them before me,
trampled them into living stairs
that whimpered softly
as I climbed and left each one behind.

"Come as you are," the preacher said,
as we stood, finally,
face to face.

And
I caught a reflection
of what I had become in the journey,
and I no longer knew myself,
at all.

Proper 13/18

> But now you must get rid of all such things—anger, wrath,
> malice, slander, and abusive language from your mouth.
> Colossians 3:8

Erinyes

No one told Jael to put down her weapon.
When the enemy of the people
slept docilely in her home
dirt-crusted and drenched in blood
from the carnage enacted upon the Israelites,
nobody told her to refrain from anger.

No one told Esther to calm down.
When her uncle tore his garments at the news
of the impending destruction of the people,
when she set her spine to steel
and prepared to lure a tyrant
into a deadly honeytrap, to save her family,
nobody told her not to fret.

No one told Miriam to hush;
she, whose childhood was set
to the soundtrack of weeping mothers
and screaming, slaughtered infants,
she who cut her milk teeth on espionage,
she who watched the waves
envelop the bodies of those
who once forced her brother into the water.

When she raised her tambourine,
and her rage-roughened voice,
nobody told her to forsake wrath.

But now: the songs of old
are reduced to this tired refrain:
"Hush. Don't get upset."

Tamar's complaint is brushed aside.
Jephthah's daughter laments alone.

Reject this.
Wield weapon, wine, and song.
Affirm your fury.

Proper 14/19

For where your treasure is, there your heart will be also.

Luke 12:34

Wall

By all means, build it.
Circle the stones around your hoard.

You have shown us what your heart is:
it is lined with the gold
pried from the fillings of the poor;
it glistens with the sweat of the laborer;
it pulses in time to the stock-market bell.

You have shown us where your heart is:
it is tucked away in your wallet.

But know this, as you count your coins:
we will be coming.

Do you not recognize us?
We are the prophets of the Most High,
the original protest march.
When we circle your citadel
for the seventh time
the last of your plans will fall to rubble
and we will enter your vaults to collect
the riches you have hoarded.

We come not to steal, but to liberate,
to uplift the poor and compensate,
to march with the musicians,
and celebrate.

We will gather up the children
and return them to their families;
we will establish the elderly in dignity
we will restore the balance of the earth:
food for those who hunger,
clear, flowing water for the thirsty,
justice for all who have been oppressed.

By all means, build a wall to hold your jaded heart.
You may keep your trinkets;
we are here for treasure.

Proper 15/20

We are surrounded by so great a cloud of witnesses...
Hebrews 12:1

Unnatural

Mary recalls their foremothers—
the trials of Ruth who, by faith,
lay with Boaz against her nature,
so Obed might be placed in Naomi's arms,
securing and affirming their community.

Martha sheds a tear for their forebears—
for David and Jonathan
who endured, by faith,
the anger of a father who would not allow
those two beloveds to be together.

Mary rejoices
that their status in their town is solid
that their Lazarus was born from their love,
and not from a need for security.

Martha reflects
on the comfort that comes
from their families who affirm them,
who would never allow anyone
to send them away.

Their breathing slows
as they fall gently into a natural sleep,
unburdened by the weight of judgment
content in the life they have made together:

within the lineage of the saints
in the tradition of the faithful
enveloped by witnesses who gaze with pride
at the fruit of all their perseverance.

Proper 16/21

In you, O Lord, I take refuge; let me never be put to shame.
Psalm 71:1

Genesis

When the stage lights are lowered
and the music drops to a hum
and the young earnest preacher
prays into the microphone,
all are invited to bow their heads.

The boys dip their chins belatedly,
but the girls learn early the habit
of hanging their heads low.

A woman's head is heavy
with the judgment of unearned shame.
The female is born bent-necked,
a posture perfected by constant self-checks
of hemlines, of cleavage, of skin.

Eve was the first.
And now we replicate her endlessly.
We are the genesis of a million billion Eves
who hide their nakedness in the shadows
who stare at the untilled ground
who self-check and recheck their blood
yearning for the freedom of the Adams
while they carry the burden of knowing
alone.

Proper 17/22

But when you give a banquet, invite the poor, the crippled, the
lame, and the blind. Luke 14:13

Streets of Gold

It has been many years now
since poverty blasted the smile
off the face of the pursuit of happiness
in this neighborhood.

Empty buildings hang precariously—
rows of decaying teeth
along the gums of the streets
although a few strong incisors remain
ready to bite back.

I climb the steps to one such pearly gate.

"You're not a guest here, you're at home."
He speaks with the easy air of one
accustomed to finding home anywhere.

Here is found: family, connection,
tables groaning with food
spread out for the benefit
of the souls who walk these streets of gold.

Welcomed, warmed, and well-fed
I collect my coat. The door gapes open,
and I am spat out onto the street,
the breath of God warm at my back.

Proper 18/23

For it was you who formed my inward parts; you knit me together in my mother's womb. Psalm 139:13

Abomination

Who has unraveled you?
Who has snipped and ripped
at your intricate strands
until the very fibers of your being hang
like cobwebs across the chasm
between the lies you have been told
and the truth of who you are?

Who slipped loose the yarn,
who has dropped all these stitches,
who undid all My good work?

Who hung you out to dry
beneath the merciless heat
of an oppressive sun,
until the vibrant brightness
and the rich depths
of the spectacular spectrum I gave you
have faded and greyed into the muted pallor
of an over-washed sock?

Who stripped out the colors,
who has denied you the promise
of My rainbow?

Who has soiled you?
Who ground into your soul the filthy fallacy
that I made you wrong,
so ruthlessly that you have begun to settle limply
into this matted, besmirched
state of existing?

Who slung the mud,
who wrote your name in dirt,
who infringed upon My trademark?

Who has discarded you?
Who has removed you from the honored place of display,
slipping you farther and further back
into the shadowed corners of the closet?

Who discounted your worth,
who miscalculated your value,
who diminished My treasure?

Who has done this abominable thing
to My good and perfect creation?

Show Mama who did this to you,
I will sort them out.

Proper 19/24

"Or what woman having ten silver coins, if she loses one of them, does not light a lamp, sweep the house, and search carefully until she finds it?" Luke 15:8

Inflation

On those rare days when I clean house
I pull on a pair of jeans,
and some old shirt I got for five bucks,
so I don't wreck my good clothes.

Music is a must.
I need it loud enough
to cover the roar of the vacuum.
The absolute last thing I want
is to have nothing to distract me
from the boredom of the task.

And when the cylinder growls
with the rattle of a sucked-up coin
I'm just happy if it doesn't clog the pipe.
I won't bother to pull apart the appliance
and dig through the debris
for lost treasure.

I guess a coin is just not worth
what it used to be.

I go through life that way,
cranking up the noise
so I can ignore the rumblings
that invite me to go to the trouble
of calculating the age of the child
who sweats in deadly, cramped conditions
for fourteen hours a day
so I can buy a five-dollar shirt.

Prize of heaven, sucked into the machine
while I, a sinner, refuse to repent.

Holy Cross

Where is the one who is wise? Where is the scribe? Where is the debater of this age? Has not God made foolish the wisdom of the world? 1 Corinthians 1:20

The First Wife

You requested me once, dreamed of me,
begged for me to be with you forever.
But while I had my hands on the spindle,
busy at the task of wool and wisdom,
you were reaching your own hands out
to grasp other comforts.

You must have skipped with joy
when you saw her treasures.
"Happy are your wives," she said,
as if a human heart could hold you.

No, you show true devotion
to your second wife whose name is Wealth.
She brought you to your third wife, Power.
Together they took you to kneel
at the feet of your fourth wife, Vanity.

And what of me,
the wife you requested of God?
I was more precious than jewels.
I once surpassed them all.
You loved me first.

I cry out in the street,
in the squares I raise my voice:
      "You loved me before.
      Will you love me again?
      Will you love me?
      Will you?"

Proper 20/25

My joy is gone, grief is upon me, my heart is sick. Jeremiah 8:18

Swearing as Spiritual Practice

I endorse no particular word.

Crack open the box
of your culture's taboos,
and choose your own adventure.

Pick one heavy with meaning,
weighted with power comparable
to the strength of your pain.

Thread it through your fingers,
feel the shape of it
cram it in your mouth and get the taste of it,
the unsavory flavor of bitterness,
of all that remains after joy has left.

Then,
before the sharp edge cuts your tongue,
grind down with your teeth
until it oozes and leaks,
'til it drips down your chin,
'til the balm it creates
heats and hazes and floats
like incense from the incensed,
until it rises in groans and sighs
too deep for words.

And when you have mashed into it
the fullness of your heart-sick sorrow,
you will have transformed profanity
into prayer.

Proper 21/26

Alas for those who lie on beds of ivory, and lounge on
their couches, and eat lambs from the flock, and calves from
the stall... Amos 6:4

The Tax

Is it not enough?
You pick my pockets to gild your castles,
and I am left with lint.
The foundation of your fiefdom
is soil filched from my fields,
and I am left with barren concrete.
Is that not enough?

No, not enough for you.
Now I carry your sins
in the sickness of my own flesh.
Your iniquities have afflicted my bones.

You snatch my days
and add them to your ledger.
You filter poison through my lungs;
your greed
lines the arteries of my heart.

Beware, you rulers of this land:
the Auditor will bring a reckoning.

Proper 22/27

By the rivers of Babylon—there we sat down and there we wept
when we remembered Zion. Psalm 137:1

Hebel

Eternal dust that caked the faces
of those who wept in Babylon,
in Dachau,
in Rohwer, Arkansas
fly into the eyes
of we who ignore the tears in Tijuana,
until we weep anew.

Ageless star, that blazed with indignation
over the atrocities of Herod,
of Boa Ogoi,
of Tulsa, Oklahoma
seethe again
over we who desiccate children,
until we rage anew.

Timeless ore, that pierced the skin
on the hill of execution,
on the Middle Passage,
on the fence outside Laramie, Wyoming
press into the flesh
of we who fear no razor wire,
until we bleed anew.

Steel, sun, and soil
reveal to us new ways
of addressing ancient offences.

As the earth turns, as the year turns,
so may we turn
away from persistent evils
towards eternal truths.

Proper 23/28

As Jesus entered a village, ten lepers approached him. Keeping
their distance... Luke 17:12

Immanent

Where I come from, we are familiar
with the concept of distance.

We know about road trips
that are measured in days, not hours,
about beloved faces
aging years in the blink of an eye,
in our absence.

We humans crave connection.

Built for relationship
our fingertips press longingly
against the surface of a screen,
of a letter
of a casket.

There is something about
sharing the same air
that cannot be replicated.
Is this why you came here?
Folding reality, slipping into skin,
longing to be near.

Lonely God
moved to acts of compassion,
deeds designed to build community,
dismantle barriers, all to close the distance.

Be not forlorn, abide here with me.
Let us be lonely
together.

Canadian Thanksgiving Day

Jesus said to them, "I am the bread of life. Whoever comes to me
will never be hungry, and whoever believes in me will never be
thirsty." John 6:35

Gathering

As we gather around this table
we are reminded of the vibrant earth
that endures through the seasons
of humanity's warm care
and cold neglect.

We are reminded of land
where First People died
and still live, and had lived
long before the settlers
set greedy eyes upon this land.

We are reminded of those
who bend their backs to work the soil,
and yet subsist on the meager crumbs
that fall from wealthier tables
of those who give of themselves so we can live
on more than bread alone.

As we gather in this welcoming place,
we are reminded of other doors
slammed shut in our faces.

We are reminded of chairs
left empty in honor of those
who will not join us this day.

As we gather in this season of gratitude,
we are reminded to be thankful
for food and for friends
for chosen families
for the life-spark within us all
that kindles, as we gather.

Proper 24/29

When the man saw that he did not prevail against Jacob, he struck him on the hip socket; and Jacob's hip was put out of joint as he wrestled with him. Genesis 32:25

Par Terre

Don't just sit there, do something.

Precede me:
Show me you have been here.
Show me that you too have sent
the very best of yourself ahead,
casting your entire body of work
into the pit, hoping to assuage the wrath of an angry god,
only to find yourself here
with your face pressed into these rocks,
mouth full of dust.

Fight with me:
Show me that this has meaning.
Do not abandon me in the dirt:
arms flailing, voice wailing,
words railing, alone.
Square up against me, if you must,
or, better yet,
align your spine against mine,
bone to bone, fists clenched,
chin set, muscles tense
so that back to back we can face
the monsters of this night.

Curse with me:
Show me I can blaspheme.
Paint speech bubbles in the sky
and invite me to belch into them
the bleakest and brightest of all my doubts.
Throw sand into this fire as I exhale it,
as I twist it, as the granules melt and bubble
until these words fall as marbles at our feet.

And this, above all else, this:
Be with me.
Embody the Presence with your flesh
the Pneuma with your breath.
While the caravan of my treasures
proceeds ahead—
a serpentine river of fools-gold promises—
be the reassurance that without all that
I alone am something of worth.

And don't, do not, oh do not leave me
until I get the blessing.

If you love me, oh if you love me,
don't just do something. Sit here.

Proper 25/30

We acknowledge our wickedness, O Sovereign One, the iniquity
of our ancestors, for we have sinned against you. Jeremiah 14:20

Kaurna Country

No more excuses.

No more explaining away evil
under the pleasant fiction of
they didn't know any better,
their intentions were good.

No more evasions, no justifications
no drowning out justice
with rationalizations.

To turn away from the sins of the past
is to stamp cruelly through the pain of today
like cloven-hoofed interlopers
trampling the grassy plain to death.

To ignore the sins of yesterday
is to ensure the suffering of tomorrow,
the way rubbish swept down the drain
chokes life from the throat of the river.

I refuse to honor
the legacy of my ancestors,
while their iniquities continue.

This day I make my confession:

I acknowledge that I am of settler stock,
complicit in crimes committed
by a people who are intruders here
in Kaurna country.

Proper 26/31

When you stretch out your hands, I will hide my eyes from you;
even though you make many prayers, I will not listen; your hands
are full of blood. Isaiah 1:15

Dragons

Turn your eyes, close your ears,
shield yourself from us,
for we make no attempt
to cease doing evil.

We rip into the foundation of the earth
with our terrible talons
until oil oozes between our toes.
Our hands drip with the blood
of sea birds falling to earth,
of corals bleached from life
to ghostly death,
of congested oceans
permeated with garbage.

Had we any sense
we would cede back our dominion
of the fish of the sea and the birds of the air,
since we decline to defend their domain.

Instead we curl up to sleep
on a bed of fossils, one eye cracked open,
lest the sun or wind steal away our hoard.

O turn your countenance away.
There is no reasoning with us.

All Saints Day

Blessed are you who weep now, for you will laugh... Luke 6:21

Blest

Come, let us weep together.
More eloquent than words,
tears without reason or meaning.
Drops sourced from remorse, regret, remembering,
despair, heaviness, leaking.
The release of a cloud-burst,
solving nothing, and yet...
Come, let us weep together.

Come, let us rage together.
Earth-shattering,
ground-shaking,
teeth-aching,
dish-breaking,
blood-thirst slaking,
breath-taking.
Powerfully futile, and yet...
Come, let us rage together.

Come, let us laugh together.
Not simplistically carefree or unfettered,
but with mouths wide as the bitterness
escapes in staccato bursts.
Those who have not suffered:
beware the fallout of this shrapnel.
Heavy-hearted anti-mirth, and yet...
Come, let us laugh together.

Come, let us sit together.
Clothed in common suffering,
these tattered rags we strive
to wear with dignity.
Hands touching softly,
to comfort, to be connected.
Muscles tensed against isolation, and yet...
Come, let us sit together.

Proper 27/32

Let no one deceive you in any way; for that day will not come unless the rebellion comes first and the lawless one is revealed, the one destined for destruction. 2 Thessalonians 2:3

Day of the Law

Caligula wore a badge
the day he erected a statue of himself
in Ferguson.

The lawless one, costumed with authority,
dispensing judgment,
declaring himself to be God,
while Mike Brown, shot six times,
lay dead in the street.

The rebellion of God dawns
on the other side of crime scene tape,
waiting for Rome's certain destruction.

Proper 28/33

> For even when we were with you, we gave you this command:
> Anyone unwilling to work should not eat. 2 Thessalonians 3:10

Ruby

A capable woman, who can find?

The tightness around her eyes
never leaves her, even in sleep.
It is the tightness of the clutching of a fist
around the contents of her bank account.

The knobs of her spine are red-hot coals
that spark in the grind of life.
The bones in her feet are teeth;
they bite—sharp!—into her flesh.

It is pain that has her weeping
by the end of her shift.

Witness how hard she works
laying her body on the altar
so that you might save a dollar
on your groceries
and a billionaire can buy
their seventh yacht.

She is above rubies
and her salary is cheaper than dirt.

Reign of Christ—Proper 29/34

> When they came to the place that is called The Skull, they crucified Jesus there with the criminals, one on his right and one on his left. Luke 23:33

Golgotha

We are all lifted up, stretched out,
bodies tense, hands clenched.
We all bleed here—donor and phlebotomist.
We are all drained by the vampire's unquenchable thirst.

Are we complicit in this—
we who are crucified by debt?

We sell ourselves so cheaply
to the beast belching out the blasphemy
that this is all we are worth.

If we must be pressed (until we run dry)
between the palms of wealth and power
as Might and Money shake hands,
we at the very least deserve
our thirty pieces of silver.

Do you doubt this poverty exists?
Touch your hand to my scar.
Put a finger to the spot where desperation
has placed a permanent kiss on my flesh.

This is how salvation is earned in America.
Not once and for all,
but repeatedly, individually.
The blood that saves us is our own.

We are brought to this place of skulls
Blood and water, blood and water,
Blood and precious water.

Every week we bow our heads
and give up our spirits.
And on the third day, we return.

Thanksgiving Day USA

Let your gentleness be known to everyone. The Lord is near.
Philippians 4:5

Queer

You had been throwing pebbles at Goliath
years before the first brick
was pried from the street at Stonewall.
And when you found your Beloved
you gathered up all the fallen rocks
to build a dwelling.

He found a home in you.
The neighbors listened, wide-eyed,
to your playful banter.
Joe and Gary constructing a life.

You built a castle to house your treasures,
your riches: precious children,
your own and the ones put out
by their own kin.

How queer, how remarkable, this life,
the sharing of this love for one another.
Choosing to welcome instead of reject,
offering a home to the outcast,
your gentleness to all.

Not ruins and rubble, no.
This life, you constructed with care.

No wonder this jaded, bitter world
found you both
extraordinary.

Acknowledgments

I acknowledge the Kaurna people as the traditional custodians of the Adelaide Plains region of my birth and my youth. I respect their spiritual relationship with their Country, and I honor the perseverance of the Kaurna people in maintaining their heritage, language, and cultural beliefs despite the destructive oppression of white European settler-colonizers.

I further acknowledge that the bulk of this written work was produced on the traditional lands of the Cahokia, Kaskaskia, Michigamea, Peoria, Tamaroa, and other tribes of the Illinois Confederation; land that was colonized by white Europeans through the labor of enslaved Africans.

I honor and give credit to my family of birth; particularly my parents, who instilled in me a love for God, wordplay, and justice. Thanks, Dad, for refusing to buy a television and sending me off to read a book instead.

I honor and give credit to my family of choice, including all my e-maginary friends online, for loving and supporting me without hesitation. Laurie, you are my true partner in love and life. To my children, Laura and Oliver, I could not be prouder of the adults you have become.

I honor and give credit to the faculty and my fellow students at Eden Theological Seminary and Meadville Lombard Theological School for my theological formation.

Special thanks are owed to all those who have read and provided feedback including (but in no way limited to) Darryl Commings, Dawn Fortune, Jayson Cox-Darling, Kimberly Allen-Moorefield, Rachel Keyte, and Shannon Kearns.

I also owe a huge debt of gratitude to all the staff at The Pilgrim Press, particularly Katie Martin and Rachel Hackenberg. Thank you for recognizing something of value in my writing, and for all the work you have put into bringing this book to fruition. We'll always have Phoenix.

And to my son, Sam, whose laughter still haunts my heart: may your memory be a blessing to all who knew you, as it is to me.

Glossary

adam: transliteration of the gender-neutral Hebrew word meaning 'person' or 'human being'. Interpreted in various ways in English Bible translations including 'human', 'humankind', 'man'; and the proper noun, 'Adam'.

adamah: transliteration of the Hebrew word meaning 'ground' or 'earth', used in the creation accounts in Genesis.

adamantine: any very hard material.

adamantine-chain: chain links formed from unbreakable metal. For example: the chains holding Cerberus, the legendary three-headed dog who, according to Greek mythology, guards the gates of the Underworld.

Alan Kurdi: a three-year-old Syrian refugee who drowned in the Mediterranean Sea while he and his family were attempting to reach Europe; September 2, 2015.

Angie Valeria: a twenty-three-month-old Salvadoran migrant who drowned with her father in the Rio Grande while she and her family were attempting to enter the United States from Mexico.

Babylon: city in ancient Mesopotamia and location of the Babylonian exile, during which a significant portion of the Kingdom of Judah were held in captivity during the reign of King Nebuchadnezzar.

Balthazar: traditional name, from extrabiblical sources, for one of the Magi whose visit is described in Matthew 2:1–12.

Blacksburg: town in Virginia, United States, and location of a mass shooting at the Virginia Polytechnic Institute and State University that resulted in the death of thirty-two people, including twenty-seven students, and the wounding of seventeen others; April 16, 2007.

Boa Ogoi: location of the Bear River Massacre of over four hundred adult and children Shoshone Native Americans by the United States Army; January 29, 1863.

Caligula: third Roman emperor in the first century, CE. During his time as emperor, he installed a statue of himself in the Temple in Jerusalem.

Caspar: traditional name, from extrabiblical sources, for one of the Magi whose visit is described in Matthew 2:1–12.

Charleston: city in South Carolina, United States, and location of a mass shooting at the Emanuel African Methodist Episcopal Church that resulted in the death of nine people; June 17, 2015.

Columbine: geographical region of Colorado, United States, and location of a mass shooting at Columbine High School that resulted in the death of twelve students and a teacher, and the wounding of twenty-one others; April 20, 1999.

Dachau: Nazi concentration camp in southern Germany where an estimated 41,500 people were killed between 1933 and 1945.

FGM: ('Female' Genital Mutilation) the non-consensual cutting and/or removing of external genitalia from children who have a clitoris/labium, in an attempt to control sexuality. This author acknowledges that the terminology is problematic in that not all female people have a clitoris/labium; and asserts that this practice in no way compares to voluntary gender affirmation surgery.

Food Desert: geographic region, typically urban, with limited or no available options for access to affordable, fresh, healthy food.

Erinyes: deities of vengeance in ancient Greek religion; also known as the Furies.

Ferguson: city in St. Louis County, Missouri, United States, and location of protests following the fatal shooting of Michael Brown, Jr. by police officer Darren Wilson; August 9, 2014.

Gaia: the personification of the Earth, from Greek Mythology.

Hebel: transliteration of the Hebrew word used widely throughout Ecclesiastes to demonstrate the fleeting nature of existence. Translations include 'futile', 'mist', 'vanity', 'worthless', and 'breath'.

hir: Singular gender-neutral pronoun, possessive determiner.

hirself: Singular gender-neutral pronoun, reflexive.

homoousios: theological term used in debates over the divine nature of Christ. Roughly translates to 'being of one substance or of the same essence [inferred] as God'.

Kaurna: Indigenous people group whose traditional lands were colonized by European settlers to establish the city and surrounding areas of Adelaide, South Australia; where the author was born and spent most of her childhood.

Knoxville: city in Tennessee, United States, and location of a mass shooting at the Tennessee Valley Unitarian Universalist Church that resulted in the death of two and the wounding of six others; July 27, 2008.

Laramie: city in Wyoming, United States, and location of the torture and murder of gay American student, Matthew Shepherd, aged 21; October 6, 1998.

mamzer: a person of questionable parentage, whose conception and birth places them apart from or at odds with their community.

Melchior: traditional name, from extrabiblical sources, for one of the Magi whose visit is described in Matthew 2:1–12.

Middle Passage: the second leg of the triangular slave trade between Europe, Africa, and the Americas. Millions of enslaved Africans were forcibly transported across the Atlantic Ocean from the sixteenth to the nineteenth century so that Europe and the Americas could prosper.

Mike Brown: Michael Brown, Jr., an African-American 18-year-old man shot dead by police officer Darren Wilson; August 9, 2014.

Newtown: town in Connecticut, United States, and location of a mass shooting at Sandy Hook Elementary School that resulted in the death of twenty-six people, including twenty children; December 14, 2012.

Orlando: city in Florida, United States, and location of a mass shooting at Pulse (gay bar and nightclub) that resulted in the death of forty-nine people and the wounding of fifty-three others; June 11, 2016.

Pangaea: supercontinent of the late Paleozoic and early Mesozoic eras.

Par Terre: French phrase that translates to 'on the ground', or 'on the floor'. In wrestling the Par Terre position is ordered by the referee when one or both wrestlers demonstrate excessive passivity.

Parkland: city in Florida, United States, and location of a mass shooting at Marjory Stoneman Douglas High School that resulted in the death of fourteen students and three staff members, and the wounding of seventeen others; February 14, 2018.

Pyrite: iron pyrite, a sulfide mineral more commonly known as 'fool's gold'.

Quirinius: Roman patrician who served as governor some time at the beginning of the first century, CE. Among his military conquests was the defeat of a people group from Galatia. This author speculates that his reputation as a known villain was the reason for his inclusion in the Lukan natal narrative.

Rohwer: geographical region in Arkansas, United States, and location of the Rohwer Japanese American Relocation Center; one of the internment camps where Japanese Americans were imprisoned during World War II.

Rundle Mall: open-air, pedestrian street mall in Adelaide, South Australia.

Stonewall: Stonewall Inn, Greenwich Village, New York, United States. Location of a series of uprisings against police violence by members of the LGBTQIA+ community in 1969. Considered to be a significant moment of the queer rights movement.

The Barrier: The Israeli West Bank Barrier constructed along, and in many areas through, the Palestinian West Bank. Known in Israel as a 'barrier against terrorism', and in Palestine as a 'racial segregation' or 'apartheid wall'.

theophany: an appearance, or manifestation, of the divine.

they/them/their: plural gender-neutral pronouns, also used by some as singular gender-neutral pronouns.

Tijuana: Mexican city along the United States border and location where refugees from numerous Central American countries are made to wait to make their claim for asylum in the United States, in violation of the Geneva Convention. Also known as a location where adult caregivers are sent after being separated from the migrant children in their care, under the Trump Administration's 'zero tolerance' policy on immigration.

Tulsa: city in Oklahoma, United States, and location of the Black Wall Street Massacre of 1921 in which white residents attacked black residents and burned and looted black-owned homes and businesses.

vis: singular gender-neutral pronoun, possessive determiner.

ze: singular gender-neutral pronoun, subjective.

Index of Themes (including content warnings)

Note: In the list below, asterisks serve as a content warning to mark the themes that some readers may find traumatic. Although great care has gone into making note of those topics, please be advised that the list may not be exhaustive due to the complex nature of personal trauma.

God, breath of: 72–73, 85–86, 91–92, 112, 119–120, 128–129

God, intervention/participation of: 10–11, 58–59, 79–80, 81–82, 95–96, 102, 113–114, 121, 128–129, 135

God, mothering: 93–94, 99–100, 113–114

God, presence of: 3–4, 9, 7–8, 14–15, 42–43, 70–71, 83–84, 93–94, 122–123, 124–125, 128–129

God, wisdom of: 14–15, 117–118

Goliath: 139

Gomer: 103–104

*grief: 9, 14–15, 32–33, 34–35, 48–49, 66–67, 68–69, 72–73, 75–76, 89–90, 91–92, 93–94, 99–100, 101, 105–106, 109–110, 117–118, 119–120, 122–123, 133–134

*gun violence: 46–47, 135

Hagar: 99–100

healing: 18–19, 26–27, 44–45, 58–59, 85–86, 119–120

Herod: 22–23, 48–49, 122–123

homelessness, causes of: 22–23, 40–41, 48–49, 52–53, 56–57, 139

homelessness, experiences of: 3–4, 93–94, 112, 137–138

*homophobia/heterosexism: 18–19, 24–25, 44–45, 48–49, 70–71, 77–78, 95–96, 109–110, 113–114, 139

hunger: 5–6, 18–19, 20–21, 50–51, 64–65, 68–69, 79–80, 99–100, 107–108, 126–127, 136

idolatry : 18–19, 30–31, 64–65, 87–88, 107–108, 117–118, 130–131, 132, 135

incarnation: 1–2, 3–4, 14–15, 48–49, 60–61, 74, 83–84, 93–94, 95–96, 124–125, 128–129

injustice/justice: 5–6, 18–19, 34–35, 62–63, 66–67, 70–71, 75–76, 81–82, 87–88, 91–92, 99–100, 107–108, 121, 122–123, 130–131, 135, 136

liberation: 10–11, 30–31, 34–35, 44–45, 52–53, 70–71, 77–78, 81–82, 83–84, 91–92, 97–98, 105–106, 107–108, 135

Lot, wife of: 50–51

Love: 1–2, 7–8, 9, 26–27, 32–33, 44–45, 54–55, 56–57, 58–59, 70–71, 72–73, 74, 85–86, 89–90, 107–108, 109–110, 112, 113–114, 117–118, 124–125, 139

Magi: 22–23, 70–71, 93–94

Martha: 38, 50–51, 58–59, 64–65, 68–69, 72–73, 74, 102, 109–110

Mary Magdalene/relative of Martha: 68–69, 72–73, 74, 102, 109–110

Mary, relative of Jesus: 5–6, 7–8, 12–13, 20–21, 32–33, 48–49, 66–67, 70–71, 89–90, 93–94, 95–96, 99–100

Michal: 70–71

miracle: 5–6, 39, 44–45, 72–73, 79–80, 83–84

Miriam: 24–25, 105–106

Mount Sinai: 101

mystery/Universe/wonder: 14–15, 16–17, 30–31, 39, 42–43, 52–53, 70–71, 72–73, 77–78, 79–80, 83–84, 95–96

Naomi: 109–110

nature: 1–2, 14–15, 16–17, 24–25, 40–41, 81–82, 99–100, 107–108, 122–123, 126–127, 130–131, 132

Nazarene/Nazareth: 42–43, 58–59, 62–63, 72–73

Obed: 109–110

obstetric fistula: 99–100

Palestine: 7–8

Paul/Pauline: 77–78

Peace: 3–4, 54–55, 72–73, 79–80, 97–98

Pentecost: 91–92

Index of Scripture References

Old Testament

Revelation (cont.)

CPSIA information can be obtained
at www.ICGtesting.com
Printed in the USA
BVHW040056141121
621336BV00005B/13

9 780829 821772